Places of
POWER

To the Great Eternal Spirit, our Maker; and Mother Earth, for whom I live.
And to Denis, Stacy, Lainey and David, loyal dear friends who have blessed me
with their support and love.—*MD*

Thank you, God, for allowing me to hold the brush through which You flow.
These paintings are dedicated to Victoria, Seth, and to all the people of Ananda.—*NB*

Copyright © 1997 Michael DeMunn
Illustrations copyright © 1997 Noah Buchanan

Publisher's Cataloging-in-Publication
(Provided by Quality Books, Inc.)

DeMunn, Michael
    Places of power / by Michael DeMunn. — 1st ed.
    p. cm.
    SUMMARY: Explores with children the inherent power
of the earth and how to become attuned to it.
    ISBN: 1-883220-64-5 (hardcover)
    ISBN: 1-883220-65-3 (softcover)

    1. Nature—Religious aspects. 2. Earth—Religious aspects.
    I. Title.

    BL65.N35D45 1997   291.2'12
                                      QBI97-40328

Published by DAWN Publications
14618 Tyler Foote Road
Nevada City, CA 95959
(530) 478-7540

Printed in Hong Kong

10 9 8 7 6 5 4 3 2 1
First Edition

The illustrations in this book were done in oil.
Designed by LeeAnn Brook Design

Places of
POWER

by Michael DeMunn
Illustrated by Noah Buchanan

DAWN PUBLICATIONS

Long ago, when the world was made, the Creator also made Places of Power everywhere. These are special places we can go to where our Creator can always be found.

Since time began, animals went to Places of Power, and later the first people did too. They went there to be with the One who made the world.

All things love to be near our Maker. This is always a sacred time and place.

Places of Power can be found all over the Earth in wild and beautiful areas like canyons, forests, mountains, deserts, waterfalls, or the oceans. Places of Power can also be found in small, quiet areas, such as where an old tree grows, or in a special spot by a creek or pond.

Places of Power can be found in every country and culture too—our Maker can be found everywhere, all over the world. In the past, people often built their villages, and later cities, near a Place of Power. Perhaps there was a big hill where someone had a vision that this was a good place to live. Perhaps it was where a mighty river met the sea and the people knew it was a rich and giving place that would always feed and provide for them.

Sometimes people agree that a place is special and they decide to build a church or temple to worship there. Other people decide to leave it just the way they found it. Many other peaceful places like a park, a garden, or even your yard may be a Place of Power where our Maker speaks to us. Places of Power are everywhere and will stay forever, waiting for us to discover them.

Each of us, in our own way, has to find our Place of Power where we can go to be with our Maker. Perhaps it is where you found a wonderful stone that you will always keep. Perhaps it is where you heard a hawk cry out right above you—and it spoke a special message that only you will understand. But when you go to a Place of Power it must be quiet there or you may not be able to hear or see the way our Maker decides to speak to you.

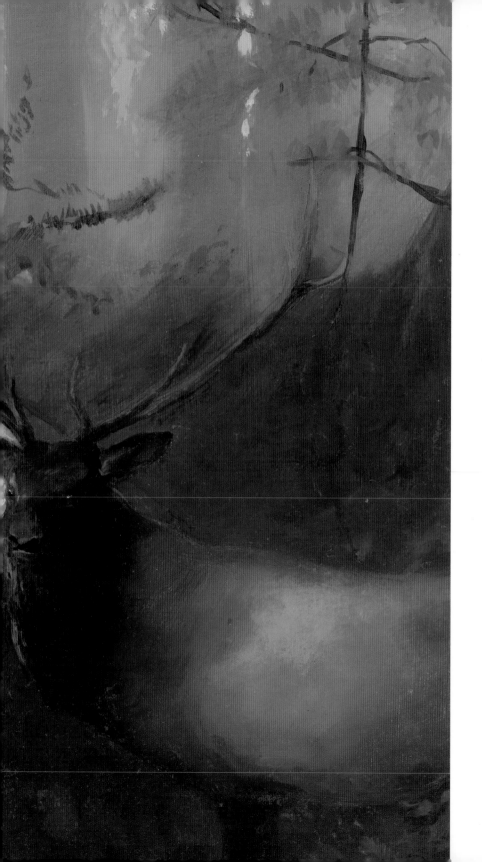

Only you may know if you have come upon a Place of Power. No one else may see or feel the same way as you do when you are there—and that's fine. This can be your special place to always go to—even when you are very old. It will always be yours to care for and protect.

When you discover your Place of Power, you must be willing to give something—such as a beautiful flower, some seeds or a special stone—to show your thanks for being there.

What you give doesn't matter, so long as it's given from your heart. When you do this, it becomes the most important thing you can give in the world.

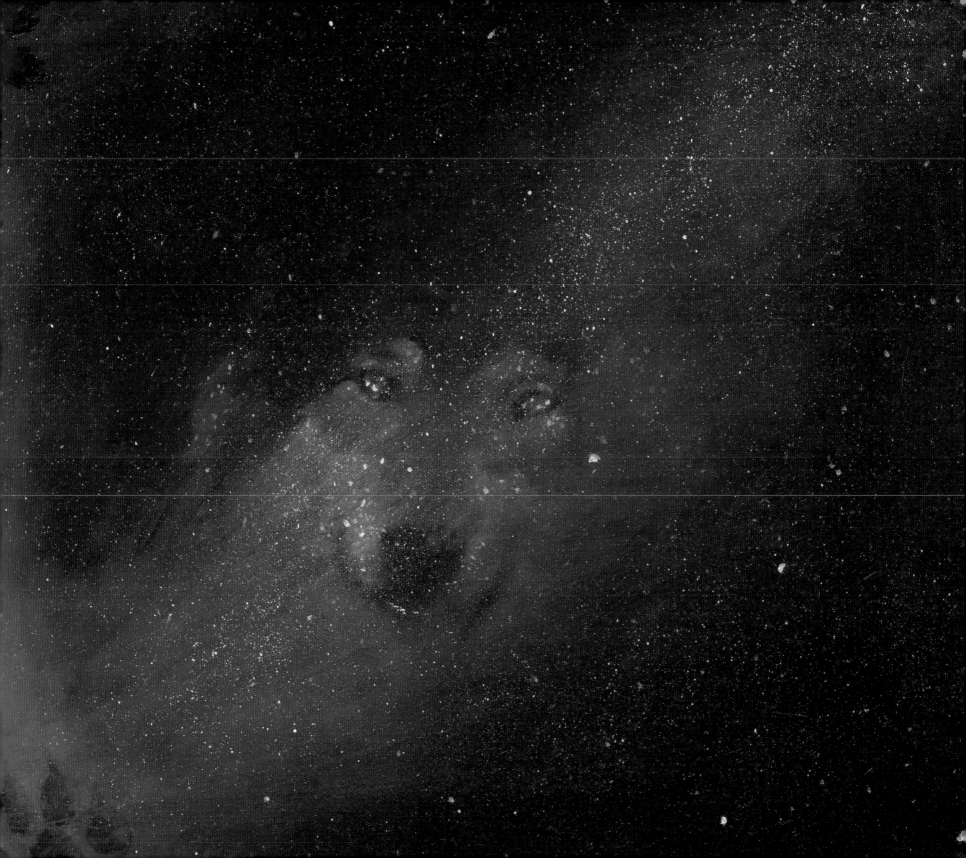

And while you are there,

Thank the Earth for everything it gives us,

Thank the Sun, the Moon, and the Stars,

Thank the trees and the animals,

Thank the plants and the soil,

Thank the air and the water,

And especially, thank the One who made them—and us all.

I promise they will hear you.

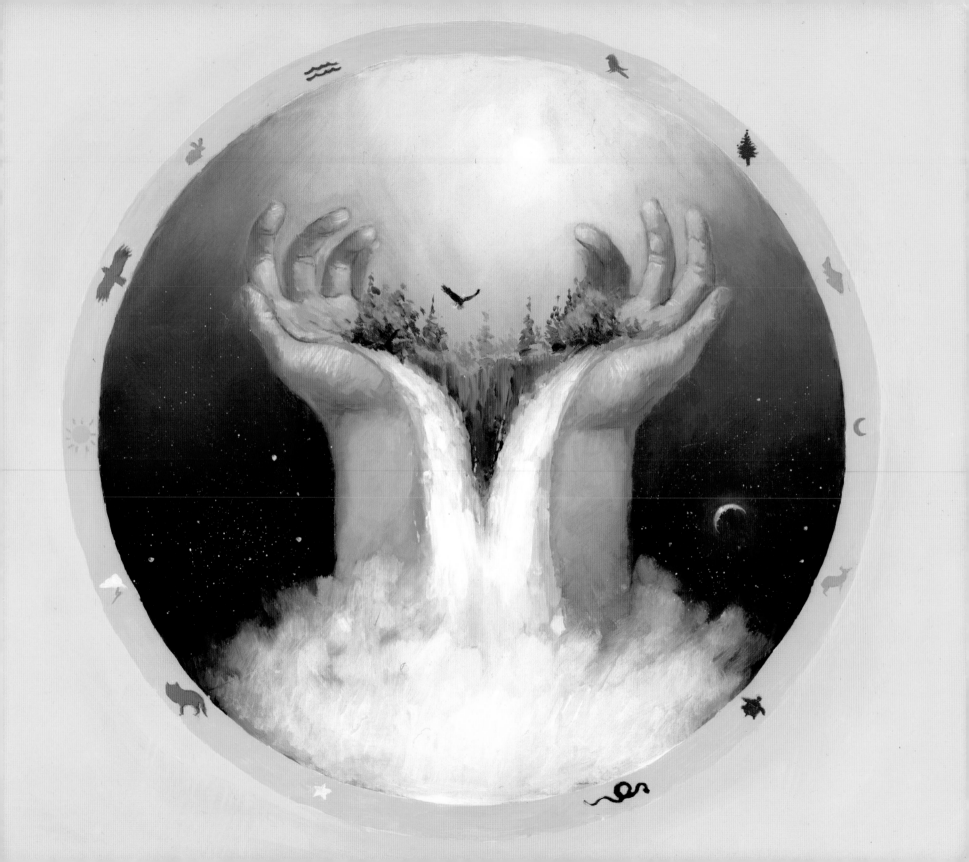

When you thank them, if you are very patient and still, you will begin to feel that the things around you are glad you are there. And you will discover a wonderful closeness with them that will stay with you forever.

This closeness may come in a way you've never felt before. Perhaps you will notice the birds come nearer to you and sing because they trust you now. Or the Sun may break through the thickest clouds and shine just on you.

Almost anything can happen at your Place of Power. If you are willing to wait, you will hear a message from our Maker. It may be a message only you will understand.

This is what so many people have done since the beginning of time. They went to their special place—their Place of Power—and gave their thanks in their own way. Some people go to their Place of Power dressed in their finest clothing, robes, or headdresses to look their best before our Maker. Or they might go at sunrise to greet the new day we all have been given. Any time or place we are with our Maker is always sacred and good.

But how you look, or what you offer as a gift, doesn't matter as much as what is in your heart. Our Maker sees how you are inside and that's what matters most of all.

Places of Power are all over the Earth, but inside
each of us is the greatest Place of Power of all. It is the
greatest power in the Universe—it's the power to give
love and caring to the Earth and everyone around us.
There is no greater power than this, and no greater
gift we can give or leave to others.

Put your hands upon your heart and feel the greatest
Place of Power there is—this is because our Maker lives
there and why each one of us is so special.

It's that simple. And that's the way it's been all over
the Earth since time began.

Michael DeMunn is a prominent forester and conservationist who has helped preserve thousands of acres of wild lands in New York State. Michael is of French-English and Seneca-Onondaga Iroquois heritage. Among many awards and honors, he most cherishes his adoption into the Seneca Hawk Clan where he was given the name "Da Hah' dā nyah:" which means "he protects the forest." He grew up exploring the beautiful Finger Lakes region and learning the wonders of the wild. Through his work, his writings, and his frequent nature tours, Michael's life is dedicated to sharing with others, especially children, the joy and wonderment of being attuned to nature.

Twenty year-old Noah Buchanan has had a passion for drawing and painting since he was very young. As a high school student he received numerous awards, notably the Congressional Art Award for a painting which was displayed in Congress for a year. While a student at the Pennsylvania Academy of Fine Arts, a painting of his won first place in a contest at the Museum of American Art. Noah is now majoring in fine art at the University of California at Santa Cruz.

Other distinctive nature awareness books
from Dawn Publications

Lifetimes, by David Rice, introduces some of nature's longest, shortest, and most unusual lifetimes, and what they have to teach us. This book teaches, but it also goes right to the heart.

Walking with Mama, by Barbara White Stynes, captures the pure joy and intimacy of a toddler—often in a backpack—discovering nature with mama.

The Tree in the Ancient Forest, by Carol Reed-Jones, uses the delightful technique of repetitive, cumulative verse to portray the remarkable web of interdependent plants and animals that all call a big old tree home.

Little Brother Moose, by James Kasperson, based on the actual behavior of some moose, follows a young moose who, lured by urban adventures, finds its way home again by listening with its whole being.

Teachers: please ask about our *Sharing Nature With Children Series* of teacher's guides by Bruce and Carol Malnor—a practical and creative way to incorporate Dawn books into the school curriculum. Ask also for information about school visits by our authors and illustrators.

Dawn Publications is dedicated to inspiring in children a deeper understanding and appreciation for all life on Earth. For a copy of our catalog please call 800-545-7475. Please also visit our web site at www.dawnpub.com.